FALKLAND HOUSE

Victor Quirie

MIRACLES AND PARABLES

David Kent

Adviser:
Reverend Graham Mitchell

Illustrated by
Gwen Green, Rob McCaig,
Francis Phillips and Martin Reiner

LATIMER HOUSE LTD — LONDON

Book 5: Miracles and Parables

Each of our first four books of Bible stories has been about several people. This book is about one person—Jesus, a Jew who lived two thousand years ago in what was then called Palestine.

From the time he was born astonishing things seemed to happen around him. But then what he himself did and said was astonishing too. Jesus was wise, kind, unselfish and brave; very demanding and yet forgiving. He taught that God loved and forgave those who tried to live kind, unselfish lives.

Jesus was plainly no ordinary man. Many Jews thought God had sent him to become the Jews' soldier-king. Christians believe he was God's son, come to Earth with a message for all mankind.

The Annunciation

It was hundreds of years since the Jews had come home to Palestine, after being held captives in far-off Babylon. But they were still ruled by foreigners—this time the Romans. Herod, a Jewish king, reigned from Jerusalem, but even he had to obey the Roman emperor. Also, Herod was cruel and much hated.

The Jews longed for a king who would rid them of Herod and the Romans. They felt sure he would come; after all, wise men said the Bible promised that such a *messiah* (saviour) would be born to a descendant of David, the great Israelite warrior king.

But no one guessed who that descendant might be—least of all a simple young working woman called Mary from the village of Nazareth.

One day, as Mary was sitting alone, an angel appeared to her.

'I bring you greetings from God,' said the angel solemnly. Mary shrank back, bewildered.

'Don't be afraid,' said the angel. 'God is pleased with you. Soon you will have a baby boy. You must call him Jesus, which means "God saves". He will become a great king, and rule Israel for ever.'

'But how can I have a baby?' asked Mary. 'I'm not yet married, and who would be the father?'

'God will be the boy's father,' replied the angel. Then it vanished, leaving Mary to marvel at what it had promised.

The Birth of Jesus

Months passed, and Mary felt her baby growing larger inside her—the baby that the angel had said would one day be a king. Kings are usually born in palaces, but Mary's baby had a very different beginning.

What happened went like this: Mary had married a man called Joseph, a carpenter. They both lived in Nazareth, but when Mary's baby was almost due to be born they had to make a journey. The Jews' Roman rulers ordered everyone back to their family's home town to be counted. Joseph's family was descended from King David, so Joseph and Mary set off to David's home town, Bethlehem.

Mary could not travel fast, and people overtook them as they trudged along the mountain roads. By the time they entered Bethlehem its only inn was full, and there was nowhere else fit for travellers to stay in.

Mary felt tired and weak. She knew that the birth of her baby was only hours away. As the cold winter night began she shivered, and miserably wondered how her tiny baby would survive.

Meanwhile something very strange was happening on the hills around Bethlehem. The shepherds there who were guarding their sheep scarcely believed their eyes when a bright light lit up the night sky and an angel suddenly appeared before

4

them. The angel reassured the trembling shepherds with this message:

'Don't be afraid. I bring you wonderful news. Your longed-for lord and saviour has been born in Bethlehem. You will find him in a stable, wrapped in a blanket and lying in a manger.'

No sooner had the angel finished speaking than the hills were full of angels singing hymns in praise of God. Then the great angel army vanished into the sky.

The shepherds almost had to pinch themselves to make sure that they had not dreamt it all.

'Come on!' cried one. 'Let's go to Bethlehem and see this wonder for ourselves.'

The Messiah is Born

The shepherds ran all the way. Bethlehem was a small town, so they soon found what they were searching for. Inside the stable they could dimly see an ox and donkey standing among the straw. But beside the animals was a man, a woman, and their newborn baby boy. For this stable was the humble shelter where Mary had given birth to Jesus.

For a while the shepherds gazed humbly at the tiny baby said to be their people's longed-for leader. Then they hurried off to spread the joyful news.

Not all believed it; a king born in a stable with a feeding trough for a cradle? Absurd! Impossible! And yet . . . it *could* just be true.

The Presentation at the Temple

Strange happenings surrounded Jesus from the time he was born. Mary and Joseph had been amazed when the shepherds came to see their baby. Then wise men appeared too, who brought presents for him.

Another surprise happened when Mary and Joseph took Jesus to the

temple in Jerusalem. (All Jewish parents took their first-born son to the temple to present him to God, and to give God presents in the child's name.)

No sooner had Mary and Joseph reached the temple steps than a strange old man walked up to them. His name was Simeon, and he lived a good, religious life. Like many other Jews, Simeon believed that God would send a messiah—a leader to rescue the Jewish nation from its troubles. Most Jews had no idea when that leader might come; perhaps tomorrow, perhaps not for many years. But something told Simeon he would live to see the messiah, and something led him to the temple that day.

Mary and Joseph knew nothing of Simeon, or what went on in his mind. So Mary was astonished when the old man took her baby gently into his arms, and started praising God.

'I can die happily now, Lord,' said

Simeon, his voice breaking with joy. 'For I have seen the saviour you have sent to the Jews—and to all the other people in the world.'

Mary could hardly believe what she heard. First the angel, then the shepherds and the wise men, now this!

Simeon told her, 'You will be unhappy, for many people in our country will reject Jesus. But to many other people he will bring great joy.'

The old man's words left Mary and Joseph rather uneasy. They knew their baby must be very special for people to say such things about him. And they were proud to think that Jesus might make people happy. But it was worrying to think that he would have enemies as well.

John Baptizes Jesus

'Mend your ways . . . look to God, for God's kingdom is coming here, upon the Earth.'

The man who shouted these warnings had a strange appearance. He wore coarse camel-hair clothes, slept rough in the desert, and lived on wild honey and locusts.

People called him John the Baptist, for he baptized people by dipping them in the River Jordan. This was a sign that God forgave them when they admitted they had disobeyed his laws, but wanted to lead better lives.

Jews from southern Palestine flocked to be baptized by this strange, stern man. Some thought that perhaps he was the Jews' expected messiah. But John himself scotched any such notion.

He said, 'You'll soon see someone far greater than I. I'm not even worthy to serve as his slave.'

One day John was busy baptizing people in the river when it came to the turn of a young man—strangely calm and with keen, clear, thoughtful eyes. It was Jesus, now grown up and almost ready to start his great work teaching people how God really wanted them to live.

John quickly realised that Jesus was the messiah, and this made him embarrassed. After all, John felt, who was he to baptize the Saviour sent to Earth by God?

'This isn't right,' John said anxiously. 'It ought to be the other way round, you should baptize me.'

But Jesus insisted, saying, 'I must do everything that's right.'

So Jesus waded out into the water and bowed his head while John poured water over it.

When Jesus had been baptized and splashed his way back to the bank a strange thing happened. He saw God's Spirit, in the shape of a dove, fluttering down to him from high in the sky. At the same time, he heard a voice speaking these words:

'You are my beloved son, and I am well pleased with you.'

Jesus' work was about to begin.

Jesus in the Desert

His rumbling stomach reminded Jesus how hungry he felt. No wonder! He had just spent 40 days and nights in the desert with nothing to eat.

Jesus had gone out there to prepare himself with fasting and praying. He would much rather not have gone. Like most other people, he would have preferred to stay at home and eat ordinary meals.

But Jesus thought he had a special task. He believed that he had been sent by God to teach people how to live truly good lives.

And he knew that, before he was fit to begin his task, he must prove to himself that he could resist temptation also. Some hard tests lay ahead of him.

Half-fainting with hunger, Jesus heard the soft whisper of God's great enemy, the evil spirit called Satan.

'Why not change some of these desert stones into bread?' whispered Satan. 'That will prove you are God's son, beyond any doubt.'

The thought of food—even dry bread—made Jesus' mouth water. But he clenched his teeth, and said 'I'll do no such thing. For the Bible tells us that bread won't feed our souls. Obeying God matters more than filling our stomachs.'

But he was so famished that he started imagining things. Or were they actually real? Now Satan seemed to be whisking him up in the air, across the desert and over Jerusalem, before landing him on the roof of the temple. From up here the people below looked like insects, and just gazing down made you giddy.

'Jump off,' hissed Satan. 'That will prove you are God's son, for the Bible says his angels will keep you from harm—they'll stop you smashing to death on the ground.'

Once more Jesus refused to be tempted. He replied, 'The Bible also says not to set God stupid tests.' (Maybe he kept his eyes shut as he spoke—you could hardly blame him.)

The Third Temptation

Twice now Satan had failed to find some weakness in Jesus. He now made his third and last try. Jesus felt himself carried higher and higher, until he stood on the top of a very high mountain. The entire Earth and its nations lay spread out in splendour below him.

'Just look at that,' murmured Satan. 'Simply worship me, and I'll give you the whole lot.'

So far Jesus had answered Satan patiently. Now he really lost his temper. 'Clear off Satan!' he cried. 'You know very well that the Bible says we must worship no one but God.'

So Satan—or the waking nightmare—vanished. Jesus found himself once more alone in the desert, as hungry as ever. But he knew he had not given in to a single temptation. He had gone on trusting God.

Jesus in Galilee

Simon and Andrew had rowed out onto the great lake called the Sea of Galilee. They had cast their fishing net, and now they were wading ashore to haul it in.

It was hard to walk thigh-deep through water over a stony lake bed, as they dragged their heavy load up to the beach. Yet they knew they must do this again and again before they caught enough fish.

It was difficult, badly paid work, but at least it gave them a living.

The brothers were nearing the shore when they glanced up and saw someone approaching. His calm, smiling face made them feel oddly at peace. The stranger was Jesus.

His first words took them both by surprise. 'Come with me,' Jesus invited. 'I'll teach you how to fish for the souls of men.'

If anyone else had said that, the brothers might have laughed and thought him mad. But Jesus had a

way of making people listen to him. The brothers felt they must obey him. They dropped their net, and strode after Jesus without so much as a backward glance at their boat.

It was the same with James and John, a bit further up the beach. They were sitting mending their nets when Jesus called them to follow him too. These brothers also dropped what they were doing.

All four men—and later others as well—set out on a brand new life as Jesus' chosen disciples.

These followers no longer earned their living by fishing or other everyday work. From now on they helped Jesus as he travelled from town to town, healing and blessing the sick and preaching a powerful message to great crowds.

Jesus announced a new kingdom— but not the independent Jewish kingdom that most Jews had been hoping for. What Jesus meant was a new 'kingdom' in people's minds; a new way of thinking and feeling about other people and God.

Like ordinary Jewish preachers, Jesus told men to obey God's laws, as set out in the Jewish Bible. But much of his message seemed strikingly different. For instance, Jesus taught the Jews to love their enemies, and he said God would forgive people if they would forgive each other. People began to see that if everyone lived and believed as Jesus did, the world would become a far better and kinder place.

The Marriage Feast at Cana

Jesus was a doer as well as a talker. Thousands learnt to admire his simple, unselfish way of living. They also marvelled at tales of his powers to perform miracles.

The Bible tells us that he performed his first miracle at a wedding feast. It was a big affair in the village of Cana. Jesus, his mother Mary and his disciples were among those invited.

At first all went with a swing. There was singing and dancing, and wine to drink. Everyone was feeling happy and cheerful when Mary whispered in Jesus' ear, 'All the wine has been drunk!'

Imagine throwing a party and finding you had forgotten to buy enough drink to keep it going! It was the bridegroom's mistake. When he

found out, the poor man would feel like crawling away with shame.

Jesus just felt embarrassed. After all, it wasn't his fault, or even his party. But his mother plainly thought it was up to him to solve the problem.

Mary looked pleadingly at her son. At first he only said, 'I cannot help. It's too soon for me to start performing miracles.'

But Mary just smiled and told the servants to do whatever he said.

Jesus saw he was beaten. So he pointed to six huge empty pots and told the servants to fill them with water. Then he told them to offer the master of ceremonies a drink from one of the pots.

The man took a sip, shut his eyes and beamed with pleasure—the water had turned into wine!

'Magnificent stuff!' he cried, slapping the bridegroom on the back. 'Party hosts usually serve up the best wine first and save the worst wine for the end when everyone is too drunk or full to care. But you have kept the best till last.'

Mary smiled proudly at Jesus. His disciples had also seen what happened, and from then on they looked at their leader with a new and even greater respect.

Nowadays not everyone believes that miracles happened as simply as this, if at all. But Jesus was such a remarkable person, it's hardly surprising if people thought he had simply to be there, to make the impossible happen.

Jesus and Zacchaeus

Wherever he went, Jesus gathered huge crowds. People came to hear his teaching, and maybe hoped to see some kind of miracle—for tales of his powers began to spread throughout Galilee.

Sometimes the crowd was so thick that those at the back could not see him at all. It was like this when Jesus was passing through the city of Jericho.

One man there, too short to look over the heads of those in front, was Zacchaeus. But Zacchaeus was determined not to miss seeing Jesus. So he ran on ahead of the crowd and climbed a tree overhanging the road.

It was pleasantly shady, but his muscles grew stiffer the longer he stayed up the tree. After a while Zacchaeus felt almost too stiff to move. Then he heard a great murmuring sound like waves sliding back down a pebbly beach, the crowd was coming! At once Zacchaeus forgot all about his aching muscles.

Soon he could see the great throng of people surrounding Jesus as he slowly paced down the road. Why, there were thousands of people! The whole city had turned out to glimpse the great teacher.

Zacchaeus felt a thrill of excitement. He hardly dared breathe as Jesus passed directly beneath him.

Then his heart missed a beat, for Jesus stopped, peered up through the leaves, and said, 'Come down, Zacchaeus. I'd like to take a rest in your house today.'

He'd said 'Zacchaeus'! Jesus had called him by name! Yet they had never met. How did Jesus know who he was? It seemed incredible.

Zacchaeus slid down that tree so fast he almost scraped the skin off his hands. Then, proudly and joyfully, he led Jesus to his home.

After this the crowd sounded rather less friendly. They disliked Zacchaeus, and with some reason; he was a Jew who had made himself rich by gathering taxes for the Jews' hated rulers, the Romans.

A Change of Heart

As people grudgingly stepped aside to let him pass, Zacchaeus heard someone mutter, 'Fancy Jesus wanting to stay with that evil man!'

But Zacchaeus suddenly knew he had changed. Meeting Jesus had done it. Jesus was poor, but his faith made him noble, calm and contented. It proved to Zacchaeus that making money no longer mattered.

'Lord,' he said humbly to Jesus, 'From now on I'll give half my wealth to the poor and if I find I've over-taxed anyone, I'll pay him back out of my own pocket—yes, I'll give him four times what he paid me.'

Jesus smiled and said to everyone looking on, 'This man was lost to God, but now he is saved. I have come to find and save lost souls just like his.'

The Prodigal Son

Some Jewish religious leaders disliked Jesus for mixing with dishonest and disreputable people. But Jesus argued that God loved everyone—even those who had once turned their backs on him, but now repented. To show what he meant he told this story.

A man had two sons. The elder son worked hard on his father's farm, with little pay. The younger son was lazy and greedy, and bored with staying at home.

One day he asked his father, 'Can I have my share of your wealth now instead of after you die?'

His father agreed and gave him a huge present of money. The young fellow was thrilled. He packed his bags and took a trip to a far-off land. In no time he had spent all his money enjoying himself.

Once he was penniless life began to become very unpleasant. His rich friends wanted no more to do with him. He began to go hungry—especially since the country was gripped by a terrible famine.

The youth who had been too proud and lazy to work now wanted a job—any job that would fill his empty belly with food. He even begged a farmer to let him look after his pigs. At least he was able to share in the dry husks the pigs were fed. He had to, for no one gave him anything else. It was the worst time in his life.

As he sat chewing his husks the son remembered what it was like back at home. He said to himself, 'Even my father's farmhands have more than enough to eat, yet here am I starving to death.'

On the spur of the moment he jumped up and headed homewards. He dreaded meeting his father after making such a mess of his life. But if he was truly sorry, maybe his father would take him on as a paid worker.

The Homecoming

He was still far off when the old man saw his son coming. The youth was a wretched sight, dusty, barefoot and covered in rags.

Some fathers might have thought, 'Serves him right.' But this one felt only pity. He hurried to meet his son.

The youth felt uncomfortable. He said, 'I've done you great wrong. I don't even deserve to be called your son any more . . .'

But the old man ignored him and shouted to his servants, 'Bring the lad the best robe in the house. Get a jewelled ring for his hand, and find him some shoes. Then kill that calf we've been fattening. Let's celebrate with a feast!'

The elder brother said grumpily, 'I work hard for next to nothing, yet when this spendthrift comes home you make a great fuss of him.'

'So we should,' said his father. 'It's as if your brother had come back from the dead. He was lost and we've found him again!'

The Good Samaritan

People often asked Jesus questions. Some would have baffled you or me, but he always found a wise answer. Often his answer took the shape of a story made up on the spot.

One day an expert in the laws of the Bible stood up at a meeting and asked Jesus this question:

'Teacher, what must I do to win a place in Heaven forever?'

Jesus knew the man was testing him, to see if what he taught fitted in with the laws laid down long ago in the Jewish Bible.

Jesus was not to be caught out. He asked another question in return: 'What does the law of Moses say you should do?'

The man replied, 'It says you must love God with all your heart, soul, strength and mind. And you must

love your neighbour as much as you love yourself.'

'That's right,' said Jesus.

But the expert pretended not to know quite what this meant. 'Who exactly *is* my neighbour?' was his next question.

Jesus felt he could best explain by telling the following story.

A Jew was making a trip from Jerusalem to Jericho. Part of the road was rough, steep and dangerous. Robbers were likely to lay in wait for lonely travellers here.

And that is exactly what happened. One moment the Jew was quietly plodding along in the hot sun. The next instant bandits leapt out from behind a rock and attacked him. They stole his money, ripped the clothes off his back and beat him up. Then they ran off, leaving him lying half dead by the road.

The Three Travellers
The wretched man was bleeding and bruised from head to toe, and a blow on the head had left him almost knocked out. For a time all he heard was a ringing noise in his head and the buzzing of flies.

Then came the sound of footsteps approaching. His eyes opened wide with fear—maybe it was the robbers returning to finish him off.

He sighed with relief to see a Jewish priest coming—help at last.

Or was it? The priest took one look at the wretch sprawled by the road and covered in blood and dust.

Then he crossed over to avoid him, and walked on quickly. Moses' law said priests must not touch blood.

Soon after, along came one of the priests' helpers. He, at least, paused and looked down at the injured man. But he knew he would get dirty and smeared with blood if he tried to clean up the poor fellow. So he also hurried off without helping.

Two men supposed to be good and kind had selfishly gone on, rather than put themselves out by stopping to aid a stranger in need.

More minutes dragged by, and the robbers' victim still lay unable to move. Then he heard the clip clop of hooves, as along came a donkey. On its back sat a Samaritan.

Now Jews and Samaritans hated each other like poison, so you would hardly expect a Samaritan to feel sorry for the Jew on the ground. But this man was different. He leapt off his donkey and knelt down beside the Jew, dabbing his wounds with something soothing, and bandaging the worst of his cuts.

Then the Samaritan lifted the Jew on to his own donkey, and walked beside it until they came to an inn.

Next day the Samaritan left, but first he paid the innkeeper to care for the Jew until he was better.

Jesus ended his story by asking, 'Now which of these three was a true neighbour to the injured man?'

'The one who helped him,' answered the expert in Bible law.

'Do as he did, then,' said Jesus.

The Sermon on the Mount

One day Jesus gave the most important speech of his life to a huge crowd. His sermon, preached on a hill, went something like this:

'Happy are the poor, the humble, the kind, the peacemakers, and those who try to be good and just—even mourners and those who are persecuted. For people like these will find their reward in the Kingdom of Heaven. The reward will be especially great for those who teach and obey God's laws.

'It's time we updated the old laws.

It is not enough just to *do* the right things, you must *think* and *feel* them as well. And when you do good, don't show off about it.

'The old laws say repay violence with violence. But I say never hit back. Love your enemies, not just your friends. If someone hurts you forgive him, and don't criticize other people. Always behave to others as you would like them to behave towards you.

'If you wish to please God you must do all this—yes, and stop wanting to collect possessions, too.'

The crowd listened amazed. For Jesus did not teach like a priest quoting the Bible; his words seemed to come straight from God.